# ALL THE BEST COOKIES

ALL THE BEST

# COOKIES

BY

## JOIE WARNER

**HEARST BOOKS • New York**

A FLAVOR BOOK

LIBRARY OF CONGRESS CATALOGING-IN-PUBLICATION DATA
Warner, Joie.
    All the best cookies/by Joie Warner.
    p.    cm.
Includes index.
ISBN 0-688-13346-0
1. Cookies.    I. Title
TX772.W357    1994
641.8'654--dc20                          94-20767
                                         CIP

*Printed in the United States of America*
10 9 8 7 6 5 4 3 2 1

*This book was created and produced by*

Flavor Publications, Inc.
208 East 51st Street, Suite 240
New York, New York 10022

# ACKNOWLEDGMENTS

THANKS TO all my cookie tasters and testers, Sarah Best, Susan Allen, Debbie Fine, Amy Lee, Maura Segal, Louise and Thom Northrop, Paul Paganelli, Sharee Fiore, Kathleen Johnson, Annie Hogan, Marcia Lowther, Susan Grant, and Rosalee MacNeil.

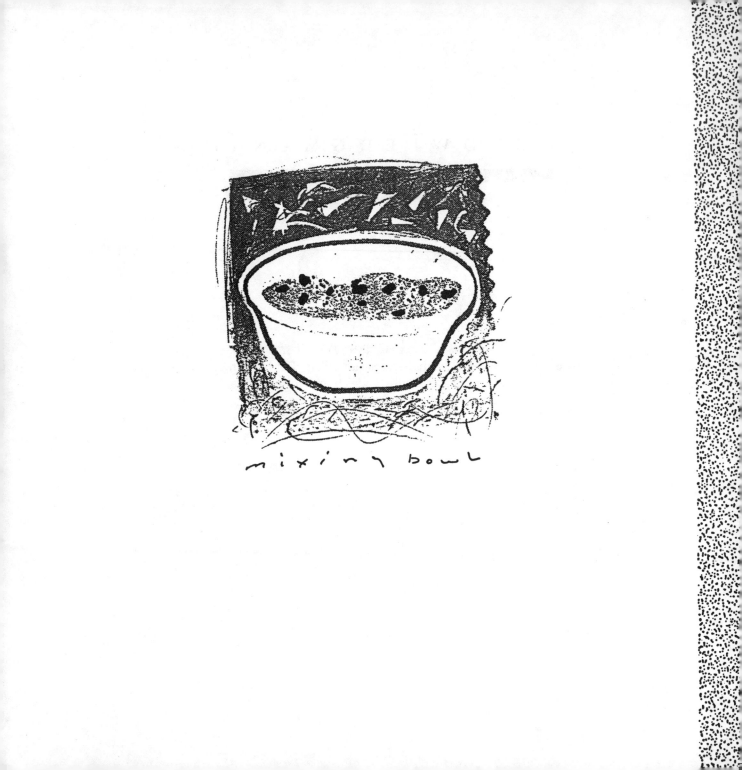

mixing bowl

# CONTENTS

# INTRODUCTION

NOTHING BUT NOTHING beats home-made, fresh-from-the-oven, honest-to-goodness, great-tasting cookies! And nothing draws people into the kitchen faster than the heady aroma of cookies cooling on the counter.

Remember that song about magic moments and love? I figure whoever wrote those lyrics had cookies in mind – if not in hand. Cookies and magical moments are inextricably entwined in the memories of my mind, like climbing roses on a white picket fence. Did you know that the sense of smell is the oldest and strongest of our senses? That's why the aroma of freshly baked cookies transports us back to childhood faster than a flash. The time-honored comfort of milk and cookies conjures up memories of getting ready for bed, snuggled up in pajamas; of returning home from school, out of breath from the run; of nursing a cold, wrapped in comforters; of mending a broken heart.

Cookies go way back in history and, stirring in the farthest reaches of my brain, are vague recollections of Alfred-the-Great burning oatcakes over a smoky fire in a cave around the year 878! Or so the legend says; I wasn't there. In any case, we do know that cookie is a word that is descended from the Dutch *koekje*, and that the first American cookbook, published in the late 1700s and called, appropriately enough, *American Cookery*, contained at least one cookie recipe. And, of course, our ancestors brought recipes with them from the Old Country. Still today, Italy is famous for biscotti, Sweden and Denmark for butter cookies, Scotland for shortbread, France for madeleines, and so on – a veritable "cookie's" tour of the world!

Crunching a cookie is a supremely sensory experience whose delight doesn't diminish with age – you didn't think Grandma made all those cookies just for you, did you? I'm sure a lot of you, like me, are cookie cravers, even though, in today's health-conscious age, it may be a cup of tea and just one cookie (well, just one at a time!).

Whatever anyone says, I am of the firm belief that made-at-home cookies are good for you, not only as morale boosters and stress busters, though goodness knows that should be enough these days, but also as nutritious snacks. How can something that contains only fresh, natural, wholesome ingredients possibly be bad for you? Of course, as smart cookies know, moderation is the key.

The recipes you'll find here fit anyone's bill – from those watching their cholesterol to youngsters needing a quick energy fix – and they run the gamut from healthy oatmeal and raisin through traditional teatime treats to decadent delights. From the mind-boggling multitude of cookie recipes new and old, I've created simple, easy-to-follow recipes that take no time at all.

Everyone will find something they want to try: there's drop cookies for beginners, cookies that are fun to make with the kids, and no-fuss-no-muss, one-bowl mixing for cooks in a hurry. You'll find lunch-box treats, bedtime favorites, and cookies that are great for birthdays and for holiday gift-giving.

In the Basics chapter that follows, you'll find everything you need to know to get you started, including my twelve simple secrets of success. You don't need to go out and buy any fancy gadgets or the latest electrical appliance – a measuring cup, a bowl, a wooden spoon, and a cookie sheet will suffice. Nor will you need to rush all over town searching for some exotic ingredient or other. Even the dressed-up-for-the-holidays cookie recipes are uncomplicated and tested to make sure they turn out right every time.

So, why not rekindle those old memories, and create some new ones with your own friends and family, and whip up a batch of cookies today? – just watch out for those cookie monsters!

JOIE WARNER

# BASICS

## TYPES

While cookies come in myriad varieties and shapes and sizes, they are usually classed into just a few types based on the way they are made. Here are the kinds you'll find in my recipes.

**BAR COOKIES**: Easiest and quickest of all cookies to make; the dough is simply spread in a square or rectangular pan, baked, and then custom cut into manageable portions – hearty pieces for snacks, or more attractive, bite-size morsels for gifts or special occasions. Bar cookies are easy to store or tote in the pan, and they are greatly adored by children of all ages. There's oat bars and lemon bars and, of course, the most famous bar cookie of all – brownies.

**DROP COOKIES**: Next to bar cookies, drop cookies are the least demanding to make. They're made by dropping the dough onto baking sheets in uniform shapes and sizes and leaving enough space in between so they don't coalesce into one giant monster cookie! Most kids love to get their hands into drop-cookie dough to "assist" with cookie making. America's best-loved cookies are drop cookies – chocolate chip, peanut butter, and oatmeal.

**REFRIGERATOR COOKIES**: Icebox cookies – as they were known in the past – are, as the name implies, refrigerated before baking. The dough is typically rolled into a log, then chilled for a few hours or up to a day or even a week. The dough can also be well wrapped and frozen. Once you have some dough on hand, you can whip up "instant" cookies by simply slicing and baking them right from the refrigerator or freezer. Perfect for those times when unexpected guests drop by or the kids bring home some friends. Popular icebox cookies are pinwheels and butterscotch cookies.

**ROLLED COOKIES**: These afford the artistic cookie baker many opportunities for creating some of the most dazzlingly shaped and decorated cookies. They also offer the kitchenware collector, like me, the perfect excuse for getting out all those fun antique rolling pins and cookie cutters to roll and cut cookies into the shapes desired. The dough is usually ready for rolling out and cutting immediately, though sometimes it needs a brief chilling for ease of handling. Cut cookies as close together as possible: the scraps can't be overhandled or rerolled more than once, or they will be tough. Holiday cookies destined for hanging on Christmas trees are classic rolled cookies, as are old-fashioned sugar cookies, melt-in-your-mouth shortbreads, and gingerbread hands and people.

**SHAPED OR MOLDED COOKIES:** Here, chilled, firm dough is formed into balls, crescents, canes, etc., or dough is forced through a cookie press or pastry bag.

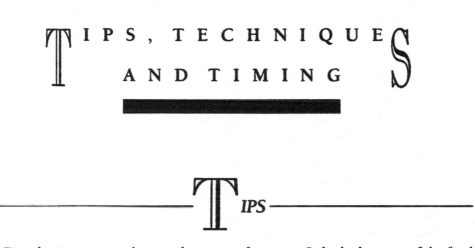

# TIPS, TECHNIQUES AND TIMING

## TIPS

First, here are my twelve simple secrets of success. Only the last part of the final admonition is difficult.

1. Always read through the recipe before you begin, placing the ingredients – in the order in which they are used – on the counter. Assemble the necessary equipment and utensils.
2. Your cookies will only be as good as the ingredients you put in them. It's absolutely crucial that you use the freshest and finest-quality ingredients. No

past-its-prime butter, shortening, or nuts. No stale, flavorless spices! Use your nose and taste before adding.

3. Butter, eggs, milk, and any other refrigerated ingredients must be at room temperature before proceeding.

4. Grease the cookie sheet. I use cooking spray, but you may spread a thin film of butter, shortening, or vegetable oil if desired. Or line the pan with foil (shiny side up) and grease if necessary.

5. Always preheat the oven to the desired temperature before you begin baking. And never assume your oven's thermostat is accurate. For a second opinion, I use a portable oven thermometer (mercury thermometers work best).

6. Use the appropriate measuring cups: a set of standard, nested measuring cups for dry ingredients, liquid measuring cups for liquids. Accurate measuring is essential.

7. Follow the recipe instructions carefully. Do not overbeat or overmix cookie dough. Beat only until the butter (or shortening) and sugar is just combined – or light and fluffy – whatever the recipe specifies. Once the dry ingredients are added to the creamed mixture, combine just until thoroughly incorporated – don't overmix – or you'll get tough cookies!

8. Form cookies in uniform shapes and sizes to ensure even baking. Space the cookie dough on baking sheets as the recipe specifies.

9. Never place cookie dough on a hot cookie sheet or the unbaked cookies will spread or melt too quickly. If you have only one sheet, line it with a piece of foil (cut to fit pan) and spoon cookie dough onto prepared foil. While the first batch is baking, cut more pieces of foil, and prepare succeeding batches. Then, once the cookie sheet is removed from the oven, simply slide the foil off the sheet onto a wire cooling rack, and slide the next dough-laden foil onto the cookie sheet. Immediately place in the oven.

10. Bake cookies in the center of the oven to allow for even heat circulation, and bake only one cookie sheet at a time.

11. Check oven temperature before putting cookies in to bake and begin timing once you've closed the oven door.

12. Do not overbake! Remove cookies from the sheet as soon as they are ready, then transfer to a wire rack to allow air to circulate freely. Try to let them cool completely before eating them!

## Techniques

To measure dry ingredients: use nested measuring cups and scoop up the ingredients and level off using a straight-edged knife or spatula. Do not tap the cup on the counter to level or you could add too much. Flour and other dry ingredients do not need to be sifted unless the recipe so indicates.

By far the best tool for creaming butter and sugar is an electric mixer. It easily aerates and lightens the mixture. You may also use a food processor, or do it by hand with a wooden spoon, although neither option does the job quite as well.

Most cookie doughs – with the exception of drop cookies – can be prepared ahead of time, then tightly wrapped and chilled before cutting or rolling out.

## Timing

Since cooking times given are approximate, begin checking the cookies at the minimum baking time recommended. Cookies bake fast and a minute here or there can make the difference between delectable and dried out.

It is almost impossible to give precise rules for doneness. There are so many factors that make baking times differ. Use your sense of smell and use your eyes. If the recipe says to cook until the edges are golden brown and the center is just cooked through, then remove them at exactly that point. Some cookies take less time if you want a soft and chewy texture, more time if you like them crisp. Don't try to do the laundry and cookies at the same time – take a break and enjoy watching and smelling the cookies bake!

# KEEPING COOKIES

In my house, the problem is keeping a couple of cookies aside for me, not storing them for later!

Be sure your cookies have cooled completely before storing.

Cookie jars, of course, are the most charming cookie canisters, but it's best to put cookies in a tightly covered tin to keep them soft or crisp. Never store the two types of cookies in the same container. Place sheets of wax paper between layers to prevent breakage. Bar cookies can be left in the pan and covered with plastic wrap or foil.

If crisp cookies do get soft, simply place them on a baking sheet and bake for about 3 minutes at 350°F or until crisp. Cool the cookies thoroughly on a wire rack before returning them to a container.

Cookies may be frozen (but for a limited time only), although nothing tastes as delicious once frozen as it did fresh. You may also freeze rolled or refrigerator dough tightly wrapped in small batches. Then you simply defrost, slice, and bake up a batch of cookies as you need them, when you need them.

# TOOLS OF THE TRADE

**COOKIE AND BAKING SHEETS:** The pans should be shiny (not dark – they tend to brown the cookies too fast), heavy-weight aluminum or heavy nonstick baking pans (again, not dark). The sheets should be flat with no sides or very low rims for even cooking.

**COOKIE CUTTERS:** These come in wonderful shapes and sizes and are fun to collect and use – I have accumulated quite a collection of antique cookie cutters from flea markets and tag sales over the years – but jar lids, inverted glasses or cups, cardboard templates – even cutting free hand – do the job just as well.

**ELECTRIC MIXERS:** I use a heavy-duty KitchenAid mixer or one of my funky '40s or '50s electric mixers. Hand-held mixers are fine for soft doughs or for whipping up egg whites for meringues.

**GLASS PIE PLATES:** I use a 9-inch glass pie plate for making shortbread.

**MEASURING CUPS:** Always use a set of nested measuring cups for measuring dry ingredients and well-marked glass measuring cups to measure liquid ingredients.

**MEASURING SPOONS:** Use a graduated set of standard measuring spoons for measuring small quantities. Use standard kitchen flatware – teaspoons and table-spoons – for measuring drop-cookie dough onto cookie sheets.

**OVEN THERMOMETER:** Even if you think your oven thermometer is accurate, it's still a good idea to double check: place a portable mercury thermometer on the middle oven rack and use it to adjust the oven temperature if necessary.

**ROLLING PIN:** I prefer a large heavy hardwood rolling pin with ball bearings in the handles.

**RULER:** A ruler is handy for measuring the size and thickness of cookies.

**TIMER:** Buy an inexpensive timer at a hardware or kitchenware shop and remember to set it! A few minutes overcooking can mean disaster.

**SIEVE/SIFTER:** I don't sift dry ingredients for cookie making, so a sifter isn't necessary for these recipes. Tiny sieves are useful for sieving baking soda, cocoa powder, or dusting cookies with confectioners' sugar.

**SPATULAS:** Rubber spatulas are an indispensable kitchen helper, especially useful for scraping bowls and folding certain mixtures. I have several in all sizes – small, medium, and restaurant size. Metal icing spatulas are great for leveling off dry ingredients when measuring and for transferring baked cookies to cooling racks.

**WIRE COOLING RACK:** A wire cooling rack is essential. The larger the better as cookies need air all around them when cooling.

# INGREDIENTS

**BAKING POWDER:** A leavening agent (i.e. it makes the dough rise), "double acting" baking powder is used in all the recipes.

BAKING SODA: An alkali that needs to be combined with acid ingredients (buttermilk, citrus fruits, molasses, etc.) and liquid to form carbon dioxide gas which makes cakes and cookies rise. Because it has a tendency to lump, I push it through a tiny sieve when adding it to other ingredients.

BUTTER: I use lightly salted butter in my cookie recipes. You may, however, use unsalted or salted butter, but adjust the amount of salt in the recipe if you do. I don't like margarine and believe it's not healthful. I don't recommend it as a substitute for butter.

CHOCOLATE: If chocolate needs to be melted, do so over *very* low heat (it scorches easily) in a *heavy* small saucepan. Or melt chocolate in the microwave using the defrost mode, or in a double boiler. It must be cooled to room temperature before adding to mixtures. Don't allow even a spec of liquid into the chocolate or it will become lumpy. White chocolate isn't really chocolate, it comprises cocoa butter, sugar, and flavoring.

COCOA POWDER: While many cooks recommend Dutch-process cocoa powder (which has been treated with an alkali to neutralize the acidity), I prefer good-quality cocoa powder – such as Hershey or Nestlé – because it has a deeper chocolate flavor. If you prefer Dutch-process, a readily available brand is Dröste.

DRIED FRUITS: Always use dried fruits that are still soft and moist. Once they have hardened, their flavor is less than perfect and they won't soften during baking. Stir dried fruits with a little of the flour or sugar specified in the recipe to keep the pieces separate.

EGGS: The recipes all use large (not extra-large) eggs.

EXTRACTS AND OTHER FLAVORINGS: Don't skimp here: artificial flavorings taste artificial. Always use pure extracts of vanilla, almond, lemon, etc.

FLOUR: I use unbleached all-purpose flour in most of the following recipes, but any all-purpose flour may be used. Never use self-rising cake flour (it contains a leavening agent such as baking powder) when cake flour is specified.

NUTS: Be sure nuts are fresh by tasting them first. Besides being unhealthy, they will ruin the taste of your cookies. I store nuts in airtight containers in the refrigerator or freezer. Bring to room temperature before use.

PEANUT BUTTER: The supermarket variety is used in my recipes. Don't use peanut butter from the health food store: it is more oily and will alter the texture of the baked cookie.

SALT: Fear of salt has prompted many cooks to abandon it, but without salt, your cookies will taste flat. Unless you're on a salt-restricted diet, don't omit it.

**SUGAR AND OTHER SWEETENERS**: Sugar means granulated white sugar. Brown sugar – either light or dark – is measured by packing it firmly into the measuring cup. Honey or molasses cannot be substituted for sugar, but you may substitute honey for molasses and vice versa in most cases, but expect a change of flavor.

◆ ◆ ◆

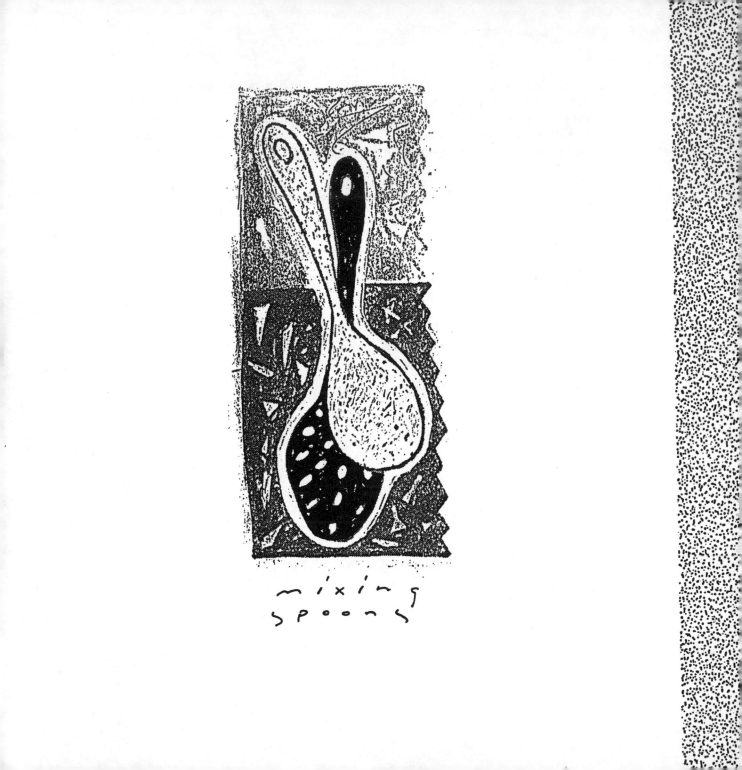

mixing
spoons

# DROP & BATTER COOKIES

◆ ◆ ◆

*S*oft and chewy chocolate chunk cookies are high on everyone's best-cookie list! ♦ *You may adjust the amount of white sugar – anywhere from ¼ cup to ¾ cup – or omit it altogether. (I confess to preferring the sweetest version.) You may also substitute white chocolate for half the chocolate, or some coarsely chopped pecans or raisins. ♦ Use the very best chocolate there is for the very best flavor – Poulain, Lindt, Tobler, or Callebaut. ♦ To make regular-size cookies, drop tablespoonfuls of dough onto cookie sheets.*

## CHOCOLATE CHIP COOKIES

1 cup (2 sticks) butter,
  at room temperature
1 cup packed brown sugar
¼ to ¾ cup sugar
2 large eggs
1 teaspoon vanilla
2 cups all-purpose flour

1 teaspoon baking soda
½ teaspoon salt
12 ounces (2 cups)
  bittersweet Lindt
  chocolate, very coarsely
  chopped, or semisweet
  chocolate chips

PREHEAT OVEN to 350°F. Adjust oven rack to middle position. Lightly spray or grease cookie sheets.

Cream butter and both sugars in large bowl of electric mixer. Beat in eggs and vanilla, then flour, baking soda, and salt just until thoroughly combined. Stir in chocolate chunks or chips.

Drop scant ¼ cupfuls of dough 3 inches apart onto prepared cookie sheets (they spread considerably). Press dough to slightly flatten. Bake in batches for 8 to 10 minutes or just until set but still soft and edges are lightly golden; do not overbake. Cool for 1 minute, then carefully transfer cookies to rack to cool. Makes about twenty 4-inch cookies or 40 regular.

## BIG WHITE CHOCOLATE CHUNK COOKIES

½ cup (1 stick) butter,
   at room temperature
½ cup sugar
¼ cup plus 2 tablespoons
   packed brown sugar
1 large egg
½ teaspoon vanilla

1 cup all-purpose flour
½ teaspoon baking soda
¼ teaspoon salt
6 ounces white chocolate,
   very coarsely chopped
   (1 cup)
3 tablespoons currants

PREHEAT OVEN to 350°F. Adjust oven rack to middle position. Lightly spray or grease cookie sheets.

Cream butter and both sugars in large bowl of electric mixer. Beat in egg and vanilla, then flour, baking soda, and salt just until thoroughly combined. Stir in white chocolate chunks and currants.

Drop scant ¼ cupfuls of dough 3 inches apart onto prepared cookie sheets (they spread considerably). Press dough to slightly flatten. Bake in batches for 8 to 10 minutes or just until set but still soft and edges are lightly golden; do not overbake. Transfer cookies to rack to cool. Makes about ten 4-inch cookies or 20 regular.

U*pscale chocolate chip cookies made with chunky chunks of white chocolate and currants. Coarsely chopped pecans may be substituted for the currants.*

♦ *The recipe can easily be doubled if desired.* ♦ *To make regular-size cookies, drop rounded teaspoonfuls of dough onto cookie sheets; shorten baking time.*

In days of yore, cooks added mashed potatoes to all manner of baked goods to keep them moist. ♦ For a double shot of chocolate, simply frost the cookies with your favorite chocolate frosting.

P o t a t o e s

## CHOCOLATE-POTATO DROP COOKIES

½ cup (1 stick) butter, at room temperature
1 cup packed brown sugar
1 large egg
1 teaspoon vanilla
2 ounces (2 squares) unsweetened chocolate, melted, cooled

½ cup unseasoned mashed potatoes (about 1 medium russet), cooled
1½ cups all-purpose flour
½ teaspoon salt
½ teaspoon baking soda
¾ cup buttermilk
1 cup currants

PREHEAT OVEN to 350°F. Adjust oven rack to middle position. Lightly spray or grease cookie sheets.

Cream butter and brown sugar in large bowl of electric mixer. Beat in egg, vanilla, melted chocolate, and potatoes until blended. Combine flour, salt, and baking soda in medium bowl.

On low speed, beat in flour mixture and buttermilk alternately just until well combined. Stir in currants.

Drop rounded tablespoonfuls of dough 1 inch apart onto prepared cookie sheets. Bake in batches for 8 to 10 minutes or just until set but still soft; do not overbake. Transfer cookies to rack to cool. Makes about 3½ dozen cookies.

## LEMON THINS

/2 cup (1 stick) butter,
  at room temperature
⅔ cup sugar
Grated zest of 1 large lemon
2 tablespoons fresh
  lemon juice
1 large egg

¼ teaspoon pure lemon
  extract
¾ cup all-purpose flour
¼ teaspoon baking powder
¼ teaspoon salt

PREHEAT OVEN to 350°F. Adjust oven rack to middle position. Lightly spray or grease cookie sheets.

Cream butter and sugar in large bowl of electric mixer. Beat in lemon zest, lemon juice, egg, and lemon extract, then flour, baking powder, and salt just until thoroughly combined.

Drop heaping tablespoonfuls of batter 4 inches apart onto prepared cookie sheets – only 4 at a time – they spread considerably and if they touch, the edges won't brown and crisp. Press dough to slightly flatten. Bake in batches for 6 to 8 minutes or just until set but still soft and edges are browned and crisp. Transfer cookies to rack to cool. Makes about ten 4-inch cookies.

Lemony Lemon Thins are one of my favorite favorites. ◆ Soft and chewy in the center, with thin, crisp, brown edges, these elegant cookies are best the day they're made. (Don't worry, they'll be gone the moment they're out of the oven!)

Delightful bitefuls! Meringues are marvelous with tea or coffee and simply sensational with sweetened sliced strawberries and whipped cream, or with after-dinner port. ◆ I like to bake my meringues until dry on the outside but still slightly moist on the inside for a wonderfully chewy, marshmallow-like interior. ◆ Don't make meringues on a humid day. Be sure to store them – once they are completely cooled – in an airtight container at room temperature.

## PECAN MERINGUES

3 large egg whites
¼ teaspoon cream of tartar
⅛ teaspoon salt
1 teaspoon vanilla

1 cup sugar
½ cup pecan halves, lightly toasted, finely chopped

PREHEAT OVEN to 300°F. Adjust oven rack to middle position. Line cookie sheets with foil or parchment paper.

Beat egg whites in large bowl of electric mixer on high speed until very soft peaks form (they tip over slightly). Add cream of tartar, salt, and vanilla and beat several seconds to combine. Beat in sugar, 1 tablespoon at a time, until very stiff peaks form. Gently fold in nuts.

Drop rounded teaspoonfuls of batter 1 inch apart onto prepared baking sheets (use fingers or another spoon to scrape off spoon), then drop another teaspoonful on top of each one, allowing high peaks and swirls to form as you scrape mixture off spoon. (Or you may use a pastry bag with large star tip to form meringues.) Reduce heat to 250°F, and bake in batches for 45 minutes or until very pale colored and dry on the outside but still moist on the inside. Makes about 2 dozen cookies.

## BUTTERY OATMEAL THINS

½ cup (1 stick) butter,
   at room temperature
½ cup sugar
½ cup packed brown sugar
1 large egg

1 teaspoon vanilla
¾ cup quick oats
   (not instant)
½ cup all-purpose flour
½ teaspoon salt

PREHEAT OVEN to 350°F. Adjust oven rack to middle position. Lightly spray or grease cookie sheets.

Cream butter and both sugars in large bowl of electric mixer. Beat in egg and vanilla, then oats, flour, and salt just until thoroughly combined.

Drop heaping tablespoonfuls of dough 4 inches apart onto prepared cookie sheets – only 4 at time – they spread considerably. Bake in batches for 6 to 8 minutes or just until set but still soft and edges are crisp and browned; do not overbake. Cool for several seconds then, using a large flat metal spatula, very carefully transfer cookies to rack to cool. Makes about 1 dozen large cookies.

Y ummy! Thin and chewy with delightfully crisp edges, I believe these to be the absolute ultimate in oatmeal cookies.

2 5

*Contributed by my friend Sarah Best, these classic, good-for-you oatmeal cookies are loaded with sun-filled raisins.*

## OATMEAL RAISIN COOKIES

½ cup (1 stick) butter,
   at room temperature
½ cup sugar
½ cup packed brown sugar
1 large egg
1 teaspoon vanilla
1 cup all-purpose flour

1 cup quick oats
   (not instant)
½ teaspoon baking powder
½ teaspoon baking soda
⅛ teaspoon salt
1 ½ cups raisins

PREHEAT OVEN to 350°F. Adjust oven rack to middle position. Lightly spray or grease cookie sheets.

Cream butter and both sugars in large bowl of electric mixer. Beat in egg and vanilla, then flour, oats, baking powder, baking soda, and salt just until thoroughly combined. Stir in raisins.

Drop heaping tablespoonfuls of dough 2 inches apart onto prepared cookie sheets. Bake in batches for 10 to 12 minutes or just until set but still soft and edges are lightly golden; do not overbake. Transfer cookies to rack to cool. Makes about 2½ dozen cookies.

## ALMOND ORANGE TUILES

2 large egg whites, at
   room temperature
6 tablespoons sugar
¼ cup (½ stick) butter,
   melted, cooled
Finely grated zest of
   1 small orange

⅛ teaspoon salt
½ cup all-purpose flour
2 generous tablespoons
   sliced almonds

PREHEAT OVEN to 350°F. Adjust oven rack to middle position. Line cookie sheet with foil, then generously spray or grease.

Beat egg whites in large bowl of electric mixer until foamy. Beat in sugar, 1 tablespoon at a time, until very thick. Add butter, orange zest, salt, flour, and almonds and gently fold just until thoroughly combined.

Drop tablespoonfuls of batter 4 inches apart onto prepared cookie sheet. Using back of metal spoon dipped in water, spread into thin, 3-inch circles. Bake in batches for 5 minutes or just until edges are golden brown. Immediately remove from oven. Working quickly, remove cookies one at a time and form them by hand into cylinders or very loosely roll each cookie around narrow rolling pin. (If necessary, rewarm any cookies that harden before shaping.) Place on rack to cool. Makes about 1 dozen cookies.

Tuiles translates into "roof tiles." Not a very elegant name for what is a very elegant cookie. ◆ Thin and crisp, tuiles are served with ice cream, fresh fruit, tea and coffee. ◆ The cookies can also be shaped into (small) cups and filled with ice cream. ◆ They are a little difficult to make: the secret – generously spray or grease foil-lined cookie sheets and use new foil for each batch; smooth the batter into the thinnest circle possible; cook only 3 or 4 at a time – and work quickly!

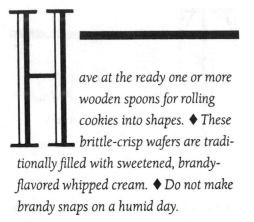

**H**ave at the ready one or more wooden spoons for rolling cookies into shapes. ♦ These brittle-crisp wafers are traditionally filled with sweetened, brandy-flavored whipped cream. ♦ Do not make brandy snaps on a humid day.

## LACY BRANDY SNAPS

¼ cup plus 2 tablespoons butter
2 tablespoons packed brown sugar
¼ cup Tate and Lyle golden syrup or dark corn syrup
¼ cup plus 1 tablespoon all-purpose flour

½ teaspoon ground ginger
Finely grated zest of ½ small lemon
1 tablespoon brandy
Plain or brandy-flavored whipped cream (optional)

PREHEAT OVEN to 350°F. Adjust oven rack to middle position. Line cookie sheets with foil, then generously spray or grease.

Melt butter and brown sugar in medium saucepan over medium heat, stirring until well blended. Remove from heat. Stir in golden syrup, flour, ginger, lemon zest, and brandy just until thoroughly combined.

Drop scant tablespoonfuls of batter 4 inches apart onto prepared cookie sheets – only 4 at a time. Bake in batches for 5 minutes or until bubbly and deep golden brown. Immediately remove from oven, cool slightly or just until firm enough and cool enough to handle. Working quickly, remove cookies one at a time and form them by hand into 1-inch diameter cylinders or very loosely roll around wooden spoon handle or metal cone form. (If necessary, rewarm any cookies that harden before shaping.) Place on rack to cool. Store in airtight container for up to 1 week. Pipe or spoon sweetened plain or brandy-flavored whipped cream into cookies just before serving. Makes about 1 dozen cookies.

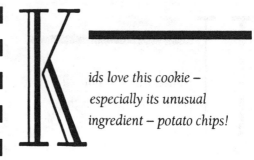

*kids love this cookie –
especially its unusual
ingredient – potato chips!*

## POTATO CHIP COOKIES

½ cup (1 stick) butter,
   at room temperature
½ cup sugar
1 large egg
1 teaspoon vanilla

1 cup all-purpose flour
1 cup crushed (not too
   fine) potato chips
Confectioners' sugar

PREHEAT OVEN to 350°F. Adjust oven rack to middle position. Lightly spray or grease cookie sheets.

   Cream butter and sugar in large bowl of electric mixer. Beat in egg and vanilla, then flour and potato chips just until thoroughly combined.

   Drop rounded teaspoonfuls of dough 2 inches apart onto prepared cookie sheets. Bake in batches for 10 to 12 minutes or just until set but still soft and lightly golden. Transfer cookies to rack and dust with confectioners's sugar, using a tiny sieve. Cool completely. Makes about 2 dozen cookies.

Updated with crystallized ginger for a fabulous flavor fillip, these are soft, cake-like cookies. ◆ For a classic rendition, substitute 1 cup each of raisins and coarsely chopped pecans.

## GINGER APPLESAUCE COOKIES

½ cup (1 stick) butter,
   at room temperature
1¼ cups packed
   brown sugar
2 large eggs
1 teaspoon vanilla
¾ cup applesauce
2¾ cups all-purpose flour

1 teaspoon baking soda
½ teaspoon salt
1 teaspoon ground
   cinnamon
¼ teaspoon ground cloves
¼ teaspoon grated nutmeg
1 generous cup crystallized
   ginger, coarsely diced

PREHEAT OVEN to 400°F. Adjust oven rack to middle position. Lightly spray or grease cookie sheets.

Cream butter and brown sugar in large bowl of electric mixer. Beat in eggs, vanilla, and applesauce, then flour, baking soda, salt, cinnamon, cloves, and nutmeg just until thoroughly combined. Stir in ginger.

Drop rounded tablespoonfuls of dough 1 inch apart onto prepared cookie sheets. Bake in batches for 8 to 10 minutes or just until set but still soft; do not overbake. Transfer cookies to rack to cool. Makes about 3 dozen cookies.

## COCONUT ALMOND MACAROONS

3 large egg whites
½ teaspoon cream of tartar
⅛ teaspoon salt
⅓ cup sugar

¼ teaspoon almond extract
1⅔ cups sweetened
    shredded coconut

PREHEAT OVEN to 325°F. Adjust oven rack to middle position. Line cookie sheets with foil, then lightly spray or grease.

Beat egg whites, cream of tartar, and salt in large bowl of electric mixer until foamy. Beat in sugar, 1 tablespoon at a time, until very stiff peaks form. Gently fold in almond extract and coconut.

Drop rounded teaspoonfuls of batter 2 inches apart onto prepared cookie sheets. Bake in batches for 15 to 20 minutes or just until set and edges are lightly golden. Cool for 1 minute, then transfer cookies to rack to cool. Makes about 3 dozen cookies.

*F illed with coconut and flavored with almond, these light and airy cookies are easy to make and just melt in your mouth.* ◆ *Don't make macaroons on a humid day.*

Old-fashioned, fun, and easy to make, these drop cookies have a soft, smooth texture beneath an attractive crackled exterior. ♦ The dough is formed into balls, then rolled to coat with sugar. When baked, the cookies expand, leaving craters of dark chocolate that contrast with the white sugar coating.

♦ Powdered sugar gives the most dramatic color contrast and cinnamon-sugar the most delicious flavor – at least to my taste. Chocoholics may choose to roll the cookies in cocoa powder for a more intense chocolate experience!

♦ Melt the butter and chocolate together in a small heavy saucepan over very low heat.

## CHOCOLATE CRINKLES

½ cup (1 stick) butter, melted, cooled
4 ounces (4 squares) unsweetened chocolate, melted, cooled
1½ cups sugar
3 large eggs

2 teaspoons vanilla
2 teaspoons baking powder
2 cups all-purpose flour
Confectioners' sugar or cinnamon-sugar for rolling

PREHEAT OVEN to 375°F. Adjust oven rack to middle position. Lightly spray or grease cookie sheets.

Stir melted butter, melted chocolate, sugar, eggs, vanilla, and baking powder in large bowl until blended. Stir in flour just until thoroughly combined.

Form dough into 1-inch balls, roll each ball in sugar, and place 2 inches apart on prepared cookie sheets. Bake in batches for 8 to 10 minutes or just until set but still soft and tops are crackled; do not overbake. Transfer cookies to rack to cool. Makes about 3 dozen cookies.

## CANDY COOKIES

½ cup (1 stick) butter,
   at room temperature
½ cup sugar
½ cup packed brown sugar
1 large egg
2 teaspoons vanilla
1 cup all-purpose flour

¾ cup quick oats (not
   instant)
½ teaspoon baking soda
¼ teaspoon salt
½ cup candy-coated milk
   chocolate (such as
   Nestlé's Smarties)

PREHEAT OVEN to 350°F. Adjust oven rack to middle position. Lightly spray or grease cookie sheets.

Cream butter and both sugars in large bowl of electric mixer. Beat in egg and vanilla, then flour, oats, baking soda, and salt just until thoroughly combined. Stir in candy.

Drop scant ¼ cupfuls of dough 4 inches apart onto prepared cookie sheets. Press dough to slightly flatten. Bake in batches for 8 to 10 minutes or just until set but still soft and edges are lightly golden; do not overbake. Transfer cookies to rack to cool. Makes about 1 dozen large cookies.

K ids and grown-ups alike adore these fun-looking, fun-to-make, fun-to-eat cookies. They're soft and chewy with lots and lots of crunchy, colorful candies. ◆ The recipe can easily be doubled if desired.

Lemon-scented madeleines are a dainty treat to serve with — or dip in — tea. Madeleines are delicate sponge-cake-like cookies that are baked in special madeleine molds (available in cookware shops). ♦ It is important to generously butter the molds — even nonstick ones — or the cookies will stick. The batter must be baked the minute it's made. ♦ Serve madeleines the day they're baked.

citrus juicer

## LEMON MADELEINES

2 large eggs
½ cup sugar
Grated zest of
   1 medium lemon
1 tablespoon fresh
   lemon juice

⅔ cup all-purpose flour
¼ cup (½ stick) butter,
   melted, cooled slightly
Confectioners' sugar for
   dusting

PREHEAT OVEN to 350°F. Adjust oven rack to middle position. Generously spray or butter 12-form 3- x 2-inch nonstick madeleine molds.

Beat eggs and sugar in large bowl of electric mixer until very pale yellow and very thick, about 5 minutes. Very gently fold in lemon zest, lemon juice, flour, and butter with rubber spatula until thoroughly combined, but do not overmix.

Fill molds ⅔ full. Bake in batches for 7 to 10 minutes or just until set and edges are lightly golden. Cool for 2 minutes, then carefully transfer madeleines to rack (fluted side up) to cool. Lightly dust tops with confectioners' sugar, using a tiny sieve. Makes about 1 dozen madeleines.

# SHORTBREAD COOKIES

C O O K I E S

◆ ◆ ◆

Shortbreads are my favorite cookies in the whole wide world. They're elegant in their simplicity, irresistible in taste, and the easiest of all cookies to make: just throw the butter and sugar in a bowl, beat or stir to combine, incorporate the flour and flavorings of choice, then press into a pie pan. Presto! Instant treat! My biggest problem is to stop eating all the cookie dough – I like it as much as the actual cookies! ◆ If you don't have rice flour or cornstarch just use 1 cup flour. ◆ As with most shortbread, you may either press the dough into a pie pan for thick, wedge-shaped cookies, or roll chilled dough to 1/8-inch thickness between two pieces of plastic wrap for thin, slightly crisp cookies (see adjoining recipe for technique and baking time).

## CLASSIC SHORTBREAD COOKIES

1/2 cup (1 stick) butter, at room temperature
3/4 cup all-purpose flour
1/4 cup rice flour or cornstarch
1/8 teaspoon salt

1/3 cup sugar or confectioners' sugar
1/2 teaspoon vanilla
1/4 teaspoon almond extract (optional)

PREHEAT OVEN to 350°F. Adjust oven rack to middle position.

Cream butter in large bowl of electric mixer. Beat in flour, rice flour or cornstarch, salt, sugar, vanilla, and almond extract just until thoroughly combined. Press dough firmly and evenly into ungreased 9-inch glass pie plate. Make a decorative border around the edge with tines of fork. Bake for 20 to 30 minutes or just until set and lightly golden. Remove pan to rack, immediately cut into 8 wedges (but don't remove from pan) and prick each wedge in 3 places with tines of fork all the way through making a pattern. Cool completely. Makes 8 cookies.

## CHOCOLATE SHORTBREAD HEARTS

1 cup (2 sticks) butter,
  at room temperature
1 cup confectioners' sugar
⅓ cup unsweetened cocoa
  powder

2 teaspoons vanilla
¼ teaspoon salt
2 cups all-purpose flour

PREHEAT OVEN to 325°F. Adjust oven rack to middle position.

Cream butter, confectioners' sugar, cocoa powder, vanilla, and salt in large bowl of electric mixer. Beat in flour just until thoroughly combined.

Divide dough into 3 pieces and roll each one to ⅛-inch thickness between 2 pieces of plastic wrap or wax paper. (If necessary, chill dough for easier handling: still in its plastic wrap, place rolled dough in freezer for a few minutes or until firm enough to cut into shapes.) Remove top piece of plastic wrap and cut into shapes with 2½-inch to 3-inch heart-shaped cookie cutter. Place 1 inch apart on ungreased cookie sheets. Bake in batches for 5 to 8 minutes or just until set. Transfer cookies to rack to cool. Makes about 2 dozen cookies.

Romantic heart-shaped cookies are a lovely way to say I love you. ◆ For a real treat, serve them as an accompaniment to the very best vanilla ice cream or an icy apple sorbet. They're terrific, too, with a tall glass of homemade lemonade, or a cup of afternoon tea.

Hawaiian flavors – coconut and macadamia nuts – are captured in buttery shortbread. ♦ If you happen to have some dried pineapple rings (available at specialty food shops or bulk food stores), dice some and add a few tablespoonfuls to the dough.

## COCONUT MACADAMIA SHORTBREAD

½ cup (1 stick) butter, at room temperature
¼ cup sugar
1 teaspoon vanilla
¼ teaspoon salt

1 cup all-purpose flour
½ cup sweetened flaked or shredded coconut
¼ cup chopped macadamia nuts (not too fine)

PREHEAT OVEN to 350°F. Adjust oven rack to middle position.

Cream butter and sugar in large bowl of electric mixer. Beat in vanilla and salt, then flour and coconut just until thoroughly combined. Stir in nuts.

Roll dough to ⅛-inch thickness between 2 pieces of plastic wrap or wax paper. (If necessary, chill dough for easier handling: still in its plastic wrap, place rolled dough in freezer for a few minutes or until firm enough to cut into shapes.) Remove top piece of plastic wrap and cut into desired shapes with cookie cutters. Place 1 inch apart on ungreased cookie sheets. Bake in batches for 5 to 8 minutes or just until set and edges are lightly golden. Transfer cookies to rack to cool. Makes about 1 dozen cookies.

## POPPYSEED SHORTBREAD

½ cup (1 stick) butter,
   at room temperature
⅓ cup sugar
1 cup all-purpose flour

¼ cup poppy seeds, lightly
   toasted
2 teaspoons vanilla

PREHEAT OVEN to 350°F. Adjust oven rack to middle position.

Cream butter and sugar in large bowl of electric mixer. Beat in flour, poppy seeds, and vanilla just until thoroughly combined.

Roll dough to ⅛-inch thickness between 2 pieces of plastic wrap or wax paper. (If necessary, chill dough for easier handling: still in its plastic wrap, place rolled dough in freezer for a few minutes or until firm enough to cut into shapes.) Remove top piece of plastic wrap and cut into desired shapes with cookie cutters. Place 1 inch apart on ungreased cookie sheets. Bake in batches for 5 to 8 minutes or just until set and edges are lightly golden. Transfer cookies to rack to cool. Makes about 1 dozen cookies.

*P*rettily flecked with black poppy seeds, you may also add lemon zest for tangy lemon-poppyseed shortbread if you like.

This nutty shortbread is jam-packed with crunchy pecans for texture and blessed with brown sugar for fabulous flavor.

## BROWN SUGAR PECAN SHORTBREAD

½ cup (1 stick) butter, at room temperature
¼ cup packed brown sugar
2 tablespoons sugar

1 teaspoon vanilla
1 cup all-purpose flour
¾ cup pecan halves, lightly toasted, finely chopped

PREHEAT OVEN to 350°F. Adjust oven rack to middle position.

Cream butter and both sugars in large bowl of electric mixer. Beat in vanilla, flour, and pecans just until thoroughly combined.

Roll dough to ⅛-inch thickness between 2 pieces of plastic wrap or wax paper. (If necessary, chill dough for easier handling: still in its plastic wrap, place rolled dough in freezer for a few minutes or until firm enough to cut into shapes.) Remove top piece of plastic wrap and cut into desired shapes with cookie cutters. Place 1 inch apart on ungreased cookie sheets. Bake in batches for 5 to 8 minutes or just until set and edges are lightly golden. Transfer cookies to rack to cool. Makes about 1 dozen cookies.

## LEMON-LIME SHORTBREAD

½ cup (1 stick) butter,
  at room temperature
1 cup all-purpose flour
⅓ cup sugar

⅛ teaspoon salt
Grated zest of 1 large lemon
Grated zest of 1 large lime
Sugar for sprinkling

PREHEAT OVEN to 350°F. Adjust oven rack to middle position.

Cream butter in large bowl of electric mixer. Beat in flour, sugar, salt, and lemon and lime zests just until thoroughly combined.

Roll dough to ⅛-inch thickness between 2 pieces of plastic wrap or wax paper. (If necessary, chill dough for easier handling: still in its plastic wrap, place rolled dough in freezer for a few minutes or until firm enough to cut into shapes.) Remove top piece of plastic wrap and cut into desired shapes with cookie cutters. Place 1 inch apart on ungreased cookie sheets. Bake in batches for 5 to 8 minutes or just until set and edges are lightly golden. Transfer cookies to rack to cool and immediately sprinkle tops with sugar. Makes about 1 dozen cookies.

M*y favorite flavors added to my favorite cookie. The lime really makes these cookies taste sublime. Try them, you'll love 'em!*

limes

41

Earthy, wholesome oatmeal adds a grand grainy texture to this authentic Scottish shortbread. ♦ The recipe, given to me by Rosalee MacNeil, was handed down from her great-grandmother.

## OATMEAL SHORTBREAD

½ cup (1 stick) butter, melted
⅓ cup packed brown sugar
1 teaspoon vanilla

¼ teaspoon salt
¾ cup all purpose flour
¾ cup quick oats (not instant)

PREHEAT OVEN to 350°F. Adjust oven rack to middle position.

Stir butter, brown sugar, vanilla, salt, flour, and oats in medium bowl just until thoroughly combined. Press dough firmly and evenly into ungreased 9-inch glass pie plate. Bake for 20 to 30 minutes or just until set. Remove pan to rack, immediately cut into 8 wedges (but don't remove from pan) and prick each wedge in 3 places all the way through with tines of fork making a pattern. Cool completely. Makes 8 cookies.

## DOUBLE GINGER SHORTBREAD HEARTS

½ cup (1 stick) butter,
  at room temperature
¼ cup plus 1 tablespoon
  sugar
¼ teaspoon ground ginger

1 cup all-purpose flour
⅛ teaspoon salt
Generous ¼ cup diced
  crystallized ginger

PREHEAT OVEN to 350°F. Adjust oven rack to middle position.

Cream butter and sugar in large bowl of electric mixer. Beat in ground ginger, then flour and salt just until thoroughly combined. Stir in crystallized ginger.

Roll dough to ⅛-inch thickness between 2 pieces of plastic wrap or wax paper. (If necessary, chill dough for easier handling: still in its plastic wrap, place rolled dough in freezer for a few minutes or until firm enough to cut into shapes.) Remove top piece of plastic wrap and cut into shapes with 2¼-inch to 3-inch heart-shaped cookie cutter. Place 1 inch apart on ungreased cookie sheets. Bake in batches for 5 to 8 minutes or just until set and edges are lightly golden. Transfer cookies to rack to cool. Makes about 1 dozen cookies.

*If I was allowed to eat only one shortbread cookie, I'd probably choose one of these utterly scrumptious shortbreads studded with crystallized ginger and flavored with ground ginger. ◆ This recipe can easily be doubled if you're allowed more than one – dozen, that is!*

C ornmeal adds a delightful crunch and subtle yellow hue to this shortbread. ♦ Why not try with blue cornmeal for a colorful difference?

## CORNMEAL SHORTBREAD

½ cup (1 stick) butter, at room temperature
¼ cup sugar
1 teaspoon vanilla

¾ cup all-purpose flour
½ cup yellow cornmeal
¼ teaspoon salt

PREHEAT OVEN to 350°F. Adjust oven rack to middle position.

Cream butter, sugar, and vanilla in large bowl of electric mixer. Beat in flour, cornmeal, and salt just until thoroughly combined. Press dough firmly and evenly into ungreased 9-inch glass pie plate. Make a decorative border around the edge with tines of fork. Bake for 20 to 30 minutes or just until set and lightly golden. Remove pan to rack, immediately cut into 8 wedges (but don't remove from pan) and prick each wedge in 3 places with tines of fork all the way through making a pattern. Cool completely. Makes 8 cookies.

## BUTTERSCOTCH SHORTBREAD

½ cup (1 stick) butter,    ½ teaspoon vanilla
  at room temperature    1 cup all-purpose flour
½ cup packed brown sugar    Pinch salt

PREHEAT OVEN to 350°F. Adjust oven rack to middle position.

Cream butter, brown sugar, and vanilla in large bowl of electric mixer. Beat in flour and salt just until thoroughly combined. Press dough firmly and evenly into ungreased 9-inch glass pie plate. Make a decorative border around the edge with tines of fork. Bake for 20 to 30 minutes or just until set and lightly golden. Remove pan to rack, immediately cut into 8 wedges (but don't remove from pan) and prick each wedge in 3 places with tines of fork all the way through making a pattern. Cool completely. Makes 8 cookies.

B rown sugar lends a sweet, butterscotchy flavor to shortbread. ♦ Unlike most shortbreads, which are typically dry and crisp, these cookies are slightly moist and chewy.

N icely nutty flavored from the browned butter, this is an extra-extra-rich shortbread.

## BROWNED BUTTER SHORTBREAD

½ cup (1 stick) butter     ¼ cup cornstarch
¾ cup all-purpose flour    ⅛ teaspoon salt
⅓ cup sugar

PREHEAT OVEN to 325°F. Adjust oven rack to middle position.

Melt butter in small heavy skillet until it begins to brown – watch carefully that it doesn't burn. Cool completely.

Stir cooled butter, flour, sugar, cornstarch, and salt in medium bowl just until thoroughly combined. Press dough firmly and evenly into ungreased 9-inch glass pie plate. Make a decorative border around the edge with tines of fork. Bake for 20 to 30 minutes or just until set and lightly golden. Remove pan to rack, immediately cut into 8 wedges (but don't remove from pan) and prick each wedge in 3 places with tines of fork all the way through making a pattern. Cool completely. Makes 8 cookies.

## ROSEMARY SHORTBREAD

½ cup (1 stick) butter,
  at room temperature
¼ cup plus 1 tablespoon
  sugar
1 tablespoon chopped fresh
  rosemary leaves (not
  dried)

1 cup all-purpose flour
¼ teaspoon salt

PREHEAT OVEN to 350°F. Adjust oven rack to middle position.

Cream butter and sugar in large bowl of electric mixer. Beat in rosemary, flour, and salt just until thoroughly combined.

Roll dough to ⅛-inch thickness between 2 pieces of plastic wrap or wax paper. (If necessary, chill dough for easier handling: still in its plastic wrap, place rolled dough in freezer for a few minutes or until firm enough to cut into shapes.) Remove top piece of plastic wrap and cut into desired shapes with cookie cutters. Place 1 inch apart on ungreased cookie sheets. Bake in batches for 5 to 8 minutes or just until set and edges are lightly golden. Transfer cookies to rack to cool. Makes about 1 dozen cookies.

Fresh herbs – rosemary, lemon thyme, lemon verbena, or lavender – add a pleasing Provence flavor and aroma to shortbread. ♦ A most interesting and intriguing cookie to offer with lemonade or iced tea, or to serve alongside vanilla ice cream.

One day I was cooking curry at the same time as I was testing a few of my cookie recipes. The cumin, turmeric, and cayenne sitting on the counter sparked the idea to add them to short-bread. The result was outrageously good. The cookies are bright yellow from the turmeric and nicely sweet and spicy. Don't be shy, give them a try!

## CURRY SHORTBREAD

½ cup (1 stick) butter,
  at room temperature
¼ cup sugar
1 cup all-purpose flour
½ teaspoon ground cumin
  seed

½ teaspoon turmeric
¼ teaspoon cayenne
¼ teaspoon coarsely
  ground black pepper
⅛ teaspoon salt

PREHEAT OVEN to 350°F. Adjust oven rack to middle position.

Cream butter and sugar in large bowl of electric mixer. Beat in flour, cumin, turmeric, cayenne, black pepper, and salt just until thoroughly combined.

Roll dough to ⅛-inch thickness between 2 pieces of plastic wrap or wax paper. (If necessary, chill dough for easier handling: still in its plastic wrap, place rolled dough in freezer for a few minutes or until firm enough to cut into shapes.) Remove top piece of plastic wrap and cut into desired shapes with cookie cutters. Place 1 inch apart on ungreased cookie sheets. Bake in batches for 5 to 8 minutes or just until set and edges are lightly golden. Transfer cookies to rack to cool. Makes about 1 dozen cookies.

## PARMESAN-PEPPER SHORTBREAD

½ cup (1 stick) butter,
   at room temperature
½ cup freshly grated
   Parmesan or Romano
   cheese
1 cup all-purpose flour
½ teaspoon coarsely
   ground black pepper

½ teaspoon salt
2 tablespoons chopped
   fresh basil leaves
   (not dried)
¼ to ½ teaspoon hot red
   pepper flakes (optional)

PREHEAT OVEN to 350°F. Adjust oven rack to middle position.

Cream butter and cheese in large bowl of electric mixer. Beat in flour, pepper, salt, basil, and red pepper flakes just until thoroughly combined.

Roll dough to ⅛-inch thickness between 2 pieces of plastic wrap or wax paper. (If necessary, chill dough for easier handling: still in its plastic wrap, place rolled dough in freezer for a few minutes or until firm enough to cut into shapes.) Remove top piece of plastic wrap and cut into desired shapes with cookie cutters. Place 1 inch apart on ungreased cookie sheets. Bake in batches for 5 to 8 minutes or just until set and edges are lightly golden. Transfer cookies to rack to cool. Makes about 1 dozen cookies.

Parmesan cheese, fresh basil, and spicy black pepper add a zesty note to shortbread. Serve with pre-dinner drinks or as a savory snack. Do not prepare in a pie pan for wedge-shaped cookies — they must be rolled thin in order to be properly crisp.

rubber
spatulas

# ROLLED & SHAPED

C O O K I E S

◆ ◆ ◆

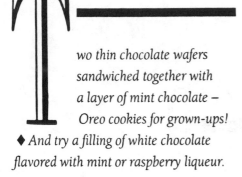

wo thin chocolate wafers sandwiched together with a layer of mint chocolate – Oreo cookies for grown-ups!

♦ And try a filling of white chocolate flavored with mint or raspberry liqueur.

## CHOCOLATE MINT COOKIE SANDWICHES

½ cup (1 stick) butter, at room temperature
½ cup sugar
1 large egg
½ teaspoon vanilla
2 ounces (2 squares) semisweet chocolate, melted, cooled

1 cup all-purpose flour
½ teaspoon salt
½ teaspoon peppermint extract
4 ounces semisweet chocolate, melted, cooled

PREHEAT OVEN to 350°F. Adjust oven rack to middle position. Lightly spray or grease cookie sheets.

Cream butter and sugar in large bowl of electric mixer. Beat in egg, vanilla, and 2 ounces melted chocolate, then flour and salt just until thoroughly combined.

Divide dough in half. Roll each piece to ⅛-inch thickness between two pieces of plastic wrap or wax paper. (If necessary, chill dough for easier handling: still in its plastic wrap, place rolled dough in freezer for a few minutes or until firm enough to cut into shapes.) Remove top piece of plastic wrap and cut into shapes using a 2-inch scalloped round cookie cutter. Place 1 inch apart on prepared cookie sheets. Bake in batches for 6 to 8 minutes or just until set. Transfer cookies to rack to cool.

Melt 4 ounces chocolate in small heavy saucepan over *very* low heat; immediately remove from heat and stir in peppermint extract. Cool to spreadable consistency. Spread thin layer of melted chocolate over half the cookies, then top with remaining cookies. Makes about 14 sandwich cookies.

## BUTTER COOKIES

1 cup (2 sticks) butter,
   at room temperature
1 cup sugar
1 large egg
2 tablespoons fresh
   orange juice

1 tablespoon vanilla
2½ cups all-purpose flour
1 teaspoon baking powder
¼ teaspoon salt

PREHEAT OVEN to 350°F. Adjust oven rack to middle position.

Cream butter and sugar in large bowl of electric mixer. Beat in egg, orange juice, and vanilla, then flour, baking powder, and salt just until thoroughly combined.

Divide dough into 4 pieces. Roll each piece to ¼-inch thickness between 2 pieces of plastic wrap or wax paper. (If necessary, chill dough for easier handling: still in its plastic wrap, place rolled dough in freezer for a few minutes or until firm enough to cut into shapes.) Remove top piece of plastic wrap and cut into desired shapes with assorted cookie cutters. Sprinkle with colored sugars, candy sprinkles, etc., if desired. Place 1 inch apart on ungreased cookie sheets. Bake in batches for 6 to 8 minutes or just until set and edges are lightly golden. Transfer cookies to rack to cool. Makes about 3 dozen cookies.

Classic butter cookies are an all-time Christmas favorite or special-occasion cookie.
♦ Delicious plain, or you may sprinkle the cut-out cookies with colored sugars, candy sprinkles, etc., or bake and decorate with frosting if you wish.

R
ich and crumbly textured
peanut butter cookies make
the perfect partner for a glass
of ice-cold milk or a mug of
hot chocolate. ♦ For an extra-peanutty
version, gently press some coarsely
chopped peanuts into the top of each
cookie before baking.

## PEANUT BUTTER COOKIES

½ cup (1 stick) butter,
   at room temperature
1 cup chunky peanut butter
1 cup packed brown sugar
1 large egg

1 tablespoon vanilla
1 ½ cups all-purpose flour
½ teaspoon baking soda
½ teaspoon salt

PREHEAT OVEN to 350°F. Adjust oven rack to middle position.
   Cream butter, peanut butter, and brown sugar in large bowl of electric mixer. Beat in egg and vanilla, then flour, baking soda, and salt just until thoroughly combined.
   Form dough into 1-inch balls and place 2 inches apart on ungreased cookie sheets. Slightly flatten each ball with tines of fork, making a crisscross pattern – the dough will crack in a few places, giving cookies their characteristic crinkled look. Bake in batches for 8 to 10 minutes or just until set and bottoms are lightly golden. Transfer cookies to rack to cool. Makes about 3 dozen cookies.

## HAZELNUT CHOCOLATE BISCOTTI

½ cup (1 stick) butter,
   at room temperature
1 cup sugar
2 large eggs
2 tablespoons Frangelico
   liqueur or strong-brewed
   espresso coffee, cooled
4 ounces (4 squares)
   unsweetened chocolate,
   melted, cooled

2 cups all-purpose flour
½ teaspoon baking powder
½ teaspoon baking soda
⅛ teaspoon salt
1 cup hazelnuts or pecan
   halves, lightly toasted,
   finely chopped

PREHEAT OVEN to 350°F. Adjust oven rack to middle position. Lightly spray or grease cookie sheet.

Cream butter and sugar in large bowl of electric mixer. Beat in eggs, liqueur, and melted chocolate, then flour, baking powder, baking soda, and salt just until thoroughly combined. Stir in nuts.

Divide dough in half. On lightly floured surface, shape dough into two flattish 2-inch diameter, 12-inch-long rolls. Place them side by side on prepared cookie sheet. Bake for 20 to 30 minutes or until firm. Cool on cookie sheet for 10 minutes. Carefully cut (the rolls are delicate at this point) on the diagonal into ½-inch-thick slices. Place slices on cookie sheet. Bake another 8 to 10 minutes each side or until lightly toasted and crisp. Transfer biscotti to rack to cool. Store in airtight container. Makes about 32 biscotti.

I talian biscotti – twice-baked cookies that are firm and crunchy – have become very popular recently and the varieties and flavorings seem endless. They are traditionally served with a cup of coffee or a glass of wine. ♦ This recipe is an adaptation of one found in Lou Seibert Pappas' book, Biscotti

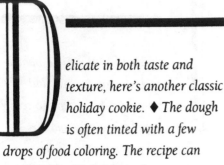

*elicate in both taste and texture, here's another classic holiday cookie.* ♦ *The dough is often tinted with a few drops of food coloring. The recipe can easily be doubled if desired.*

## CINNAMON SOUR CREAM COOKIES

½ cup (1 stick) butter,
   at room temperature
½ cup sugar
2 tablespoons sour cream
1 large egg yolk
1 teaspoon vanilla
1½ cups all-purpose flour

¾ teaspoon baking powder
¼ teaspoon baking soda
¼ teaspoon salt
¼ teaspoon ground
   cinnamon
Sugar for sprinkling

PREHEAT OVEN to 350°F. Adjust oven rack to middle position.

Cream butter, sugar, and sour cream in large bowl of electric mixer. Beat in egg yolk and vanilla, then flour, baking powder, baking soda, salt, and cinnamon just until thoroughly combined.

Divide dough into three pieces. Roll each piece to ¼-inch thickness between 2 pieces of plastic wrap or wax paper. (If necessary, chill dough for easier handling: still in its plastic wrap, place rolled dough in freezer for a few minutes or until firm enough to cut into shapes.) Remove top piece of plastic wrap and cut into desired shapes with assorted cookie cutters. Place 1 inch apart on ungreased cookie sheets and sprinkle tops with sugar. Bake in batches for 8 to 10 minutes or just until set and edges are lightly golden. Transfer cookies to rack to cool. Makes about 2 dozen cookies.

## CINNAMON SUGAR COOKIES

1 cup (2 sticks) butter,
  at room temperature
1 cup sugar
1 large egg
2¼ cups all-purpose flour
1 tablespoon ground
  cinnamon

1 teaspoon baking soda
¼ teaspoon salt
Sugar for rolling
Pecan halves for decorating

PREHEAT OVEN to 350°F. Adjust oven rack to middle position. Lightly spray or grease cookie sheets.

Cream butter and sugar in large bowl of electric mixer. Beat in egg, then flour, cinnamon, baking soda, and salt just until thoroughly combined.

Form dough into 1½-inch balls, roll in sugar, and place 2 inches apart on prepared cookie sheets. Flatten each ball to ¼-inch thickness with bottom of glass. Gently press a pecan half in center of each cookie. Bake in batches for 10 to 12 minutes or just until set. Transfer cookies to rack to cool. Makes about 2 dozen cookies.

*C innamon-scented, these lightly-crisp cookies will fill your house with their wonderful aroma while baking.* ♦ *They're wonderful with strong-brewed coffee or cappuccino or as a tea-time treat.*

butter

**M**ade with a special press, these cookies are also called "Spritz" – a German word that means "to squirt."

♦ *Your kids will love making these – assuming Mothers are ready for the clean-up!*

## COOKIE-PRESS COOKIES

1 cup (2 sticks) butter, at room temperature
½ cup sugar
1 large egg

1 teaspoon vanilla or almond extract
About 2¼ cups all-purpose flour

PREHEAT OVEN to 350°F. Adjust oven rack to middle position.

Cream butter and sugar in medium bowl. Beat in egg, vanilla or almond extract, and flour until thoroughly combined. (Test a little dough in cookie press to see if texture is right; add a little more flour if too soft.) Fill cookie press with dough, then press into desired shapes onto ungreased cookie sheets 1 inch apart. Bake in batches for 7 to 9 minutes or just until set; do not overbake. Transfer cookies to rack to cool. Makes about 2½ dozen cookies.

## Gingersnaps

¾ cup (1½ sticks) butter, at room temperature
1 cup packed brown sugar
1 large egg
¼ cup molasses
Grated zest of 1 large orange

2 cups all-purpose flour
1 tablespoon ground ginger
1 teaspoon ground cinnamon
2 teaspoons baking soda
¼ teaspoon salt
Sugar for rolling

PREHEAT OVEN to 350°F. Adjust oven rack to middle position. Lightly spray or grease cookie sheets.

Cream butter and brown sugar in large bowl of electric mixer. Beat in egg, molasses, and orange zest, then flour, ginger, cinnamon, baking soda, and salt just until thoroughly combined.

Form dough into 1½-inch balls, then roll in sugar. Place 2½ inches apart on prepared cookie sheets. Bake in batches for 8 to 10 minutes or just until set but still soft and tops are crackled. (For crisp gingersnaps, bake a bit longer or just until crisp.) Transfer cookies to rack to cool. Makes about 2 dozen 3-inch cookies.

G*enerous with ginger and with a hint of citrus, these crinkle-topped cookies taste even better the second day (if they last that long!).*

Ultra-delicate shortbread-type cookies that melt in a moment – just like their name says. Serve with your very best tea. ◆ The recipe can easily be doubled if you have a moment more!

## MELTING MOMENTS

½ cup (1 stick) butter, at room temperature
½ teaspoon vanilla
¼ teaspoon almond extract
½ cup all-purpose flour

½ cup cornstarch
¼ cup confectioners' sugar
⅛ teaspoon salt
Confectioners' sugar for dusting

PREHEAT OVEN to 350°F. Adjust oven rack to middle position.

Cream butter in large bowl of electric mixer until light and fluffy. Beat in vanilla and almond extract, then flour, cornstarch, confectioners' sugar, and salt just until thoroughly combined.

Form dough into 1-inch balls (if necessary, chill dough for easier handling) and place 2 inches apart on ungreased cookie sheets. Slightly flatten each ball with bottom of glass. Bake in batches for 8 to 10 minutes or just until set and edges are lightly golden; do not overbake. Transfer cookies to rack and completely coat with confectioners' sugar, using a tiny sieve. Cool completely. Makes about 1 dozen cookies.

## MEXICAN WEDDING COOKIES

| | |
|---|---|
| 1 cup (2 sticks) butter, at room temperature | ⅛ teaspoon salt |
| ½ cup confectioners' sugar | 2 cups all-purpose flour |
| 1 teaspoon vanilla | ½ cup pecan halves, toasted, finely chopped |
| 1 teaspoon finely grated orange zest | Confectioners' sugar for dusting |

PREHEAT OVEN to 325°F. Adjust oven rack to middle position.

Cream butter and confectioners' sugar in large bowl of electric mixer. Beat in vanilla, orange zest, salt, and flour just until thoroughly combined. Stir in nuts.

Form dough into 1-inch balls and place 1 inch apart on ungreased cookie sheets. Flatten slightly with bottom of glass. Bake in batches for 10 to 15 minutes or just until set and edges are lightly golden. Transfer cookies to rack and generously dust cookies with confectioners' sugar, using a tiny sieve. Cool completely. Makes about 2 dozen cookies.

*B asically a shortbread cookie rich in butter and nuts, Mexican Wedding Cookies are traditionally served as nuptial nibbles – hence the name – but I find them appealing any time.*

*ig, chewy, spicy cookies.*
*♦ I double or triple the recipe*
*when I'm making up a big*
*batch for the holidays.*

## SPICY GINGER MOLASSES COOKIES

½ cup (1 stick) butter,
   at room temperature
¾ cup sugar
¼ cup molasses
1 large egg
2 cups all-purpose flour
1 teaspoon baking soda

1 teaspoon ground ginger
¾ teaspoon ground cloves
¾ teaspoon ground
   cinnamon
⅛ teaspoon salt
Sugar for rolling

PREHEAT OVEN to 350°F. Adjust oven rack to middle position. Lightly spray or grease cookie sheets.

Cream butter and sugar in large bowl of electric mixer. Beat in molasses and egg, then flour, baking soda, ginger, cloves, cinnamon, and salt just until thoroughly combined.

Form dough into 1½-inch balls, roll in sugar, then press to slightly flatten. Place on prepared cookie sheets 2 inches apart. Bake in batches for 12 to 14 minutes or just until set but still soft; do not overbake. Transfer cookies to rack to cool. Makes about 2 dozen cookies.

## PEANUT BRITTLE COOKIES

½ cup (1 stick) butter,
  at room temperature
½ cup packed brown sugar
1 egg, separated
1 teaspoon vanilla
1 cup all-purpose flour

¼ teaspoon baking soda
½ teaspoon ground
  cinnamon
¼ teaspoon salt
½ cup chopped peanuts
¼ cup peanut halves

PREHEAT OVEN to 350°F. Adjust oven rack to middle position. Lightly spray or grease small cookie sheet.

Cream butter and brown sugar in large bowl of electric mixer. Beat in egg yolk and vanilla, then flour, baking soda, cinnamon, and salt just until thoroughly combined. Stir in chopped peanuts.

Press dough evenly onto prepared cookie sheet to ⅛-inch thickness (don't worry if it doesn't cover all the cookie sheet).

Beat egg white until foamy. Brush about 1 tablespoon of beaten egg white over top of dough, then decorate with peanut halves, gently pressing into dough. Bake for 12 to 14 minutes or just until set but still soft. Immediately break into irregular 2- to 3-inch pieces. Transfer cookies to rack to cool. Makes about 1 dozen cookies

*ookies for kids.* ♦ *They look a lot like chunks of crunchy peanut-brittle, but — surprise! – they're soft, melt-in-your-mouth morsels.*

Even Sherlock Holmes won't know who's who when these tell-tale thumbprint cookies are baked – and the evidence covered with jam! ◆ Naturally, home-made or best-quality preserves, jams, or jellies give the utmost flavor.

◆ Unbleached hazelnuts may be substituted for the pecans.

## PECAN THUMBPRINT COOKIES

1 cup (2 sticks) butter, at room temperature
½ cup packed brown sugar
2 large eggs, separated, whites beaten until foamy
1 teaspoon vanilla
⅛ teaspoon salt

2 cups all-purpose flour
Finely grated zest of 1 small lemon
1 cup pecan halves, chopped
Assorted fruit preserves, jams, or jellies for filling

PREHEAT OVEN to 350°F. Adjust oven rack to middle position. Lightly spray or grease cookie sheets.

Cream butter and brown sugar in large bowl of electric mixer. Beat in egg yolks, vanilla, and salt, then flour and lemon zest just until thoroughly combined.

Form dough into 1-inch balls. Roll balls in beaten egg whites, then chopped nuts. Place 1 inch apart on prepared cookie sheets. Make a depression in center of each cookie with thumb or index finger. Bake in batches for 8 to 12 minutes or just until set and lightly golden. Remove from oven and immediately re-press centers if depression has filled in while baking. Transfer cookies to rack to cool. Fill centers with preserves, jams, or jellies. Makes about 2 dozen cookies.

## OLD-FASHIONED SUGAR COOKIES

1 cup (2 sticks) butter,
  at room temperature
1 cup sugar
1 large egg
1 tablespoon vanilla
Grated zest of 1 medium
  lemon

2 cups all-purpose flour
1 teaspoon baking powder
⅛ teaspoon salt
About ¼ cup all-purpose
  flour, if needed

PREHEAT OVEN to 350°F. Adjust oven rack to middle position. Lightly spray or grease cookie sheets.

Cream butter and sugar in large bowl of electric mixer. Beat in egg, vanilla, and lemon zest, then flour, baking powder, and salt just until thoroughly combined. (If dough seems too soft, beat in more flour, but I find the less the flour, the more tender the cookie.)

Divide dough into three pieces. Roll each piece to ⅛-inch thickness between 2 pieces of plastic wrap or wax paper. (If necessary, chill dough for easier handling: still in its plastic wrap, place rolled dough in freezer for a few minutes or until firm enough to cut into shapes.) Remove top piece of plastic wrap and cut into desired shapes with assorted cookie cutters as close together as possible. (Re-rolled sugar-cookie-dough scraps are not as tender, so handle and re-roll as little as possible.) Place 1 inch apart on prepared cookie sheets. Bake in batches for 8 to 10 minutes or just until set and edges are lightly golden. Transfer cookies to rack to cool. Makes about 2 dozen cookies.

E*xtra-tender, buttery cookies just like Grandma used to make.* ♦ *The dough is perfect for cutting into fanciful shapes and decorating with sugar or colored sugar, cinnamon candies, or candy sprinkles.* ♦ *Or decorate with frosting: stir 1 cup confectioners' sugar, ¼ teaspoon vanilla, and 1 egg white or enough milk until of piping or drizzling consistency. If desired, divide frosting into small bowls and color each one with a different food coloring.*

*olidays just wouldn't be the same without fudgy, no-bake, rum-flavored cookies on the holiday cookie tray.*

## RUM BALLS

1¾ cups fine vanilla wafer crumbs
1 cup confectioners' sugar
1 cup pecan halves, lightly toasted, finely chopped
2 tablespoons unsweetened cocoa powder

3 tablespoons light corn syrup
About ¼ cup rum
Confectioners' sugar for rolling

STIR WAFER CRUMBS, confectioners' sugar, pecans, cocoa, corn syrup, and rum in bowl until thoroughly combined.

Form into 1-inch balls (no larger) and roll in confectioners' sugar. Store in covered container in refrigerator. Bring to room temperature before serving. Makes about 3½ dozen cookies.

## CINNAMON-PECAN RUGELACH

4 ounces cream cheese,
  at room temperature
½ cup (1 stick) butter,
  at room temperature
1 cup all-purpose flour
1½ teaspoons vanilla
3 tablespoons sugar
¼ teaspoon finely grated
  lemon zest
Grated zest of 1 medium
  orange

½ cup pecan halves, lightly
  toasted, finely chopped
3 tablespoons sugar
1 teaspoon ground
  cinnamon
About ¾ cup apricot
  preserves, stirred until
  spreadable

A cream-cheese pastry is filled with apricot preserves, cinnamon-sugar, and pecans, then rolled into crescents, sprinkled with more cinnamon-sugar and baked into magical mouthfuls.

CREAM THE CREAM CHEESE and butter in large bowl of electric mixer. Beat in flour, vanilla, 3 tablespoons sugar, and lemon zest. Divide in half, then form each piece into 1-inch-thick disks. Wrap each disk in plastic wrap and chill until firm enough to handle.

Combine orange zest, pecans, 2 tablespoons sugar and ½ teaspoon cinnamon in small bowl.

Preheat oven to 350°F. Adjust oven rack to middle position.

Roll each disk on lightly floured surface to 9-inch circle. Spread with apricot preserves and sprinkle with pecan mixture. Cut each circle into 12 wedges and roll to form a crescent, starting from wide end. Place 1 inch apart on ungreased cookie sheets. Combine remaining 1 tablespoon sugar and ½ teaspoon cinnamon and sprinkle over crescents. Bake in batches for 15 to 20 minutes or just until set but still soft and lightly golden. Transfer cookies to rack to cool. Makes about 24 cookies.

**B**eautiful-looking, tender-tasting, heart-shaped cookie "sandwiches" have heart-shaped "windows" to show off their raspberry-red filling. ♦ The dough is a little tricky to roll out, but patience will be rewarded!

### RASPBERRY HEARTS

1 cup (2 sticks) butter,
   at room temperature
½ cup confectioners' sugar
1 teaspoon vanilla
Finely grated zest of
   ½ small lemon
1¾ cups all-purpose flour
¼ cup cornstarch

¼ teaspoon salt
½ cup pecan halves, lightly
   toasted, finely chopped
About ¼ cup seedless
   raspberry or currant
   preserves
Confectioners' sugar for
   dusting

PREHEAT OVEN to 350°F. Adjust oven rack to middle position.

Cream butter and confectioners' sugar in large bowl of electric mixer. Beat in vanilla, lemon zest, flour, cornstarch, and salt just until thoroughly combined. Stir in nuts.

Divide dough in half. Roll dough to ⅛-inch thickness (no thicker) between 2 pieces of plastic wrap or wax paper. (If necessary, chill dough for easier handling: still in its plastic wrap, place rolled dough in freezer for a few minutes or until firm enough to cut into shapes.) Remove top piece of plastic wrap and cut dough into shapes using a 2¾-inch heart-shaped cookie cutter. Cut out centers of half the cookies with 1-inch heart-shaped cookie cutter. Place 1 inch apart on ungreased cookie sheets. Bake in batches for 6 to 8 minutes or just until set and lightly golden. Carefully transfer cookies to rack to cool.

Spread about ½ teaspoon preserves on whole cookies, then gently top each one with a "window" cookie. Cut a small heart shape from a piece of foil and use it to cover "windows." Lightly dust rims with confectioners' sugar, using a tiny sieve. Makes about 16 cookies.

## ALMOND BRICKLE COOKIES

*ursts of butterscotchy brickle bits makes these cookies decidedly addictive!*

| | |
|---|---|
| ½ cup (1 stick) butter, at room temperature | 1 ¼ cups all-purpose flour |
| ½ cup sugar | ½ teaspoon baking soda |
| 1 large egg | ⅔ cup almond brickle bits |
| ½ teaspoon vanilla | Sugar for rolling |

PREHEAT OVEN to 350°F. Adjust oven rack to middle position. Lightly spray or grease cookie sheets.

Cream butter and sugar in large bowl of electric mixer. Beat in egg and vanilla, then flour and baking soda just until thoroughly combined. Stir in brickle bits.

Form dough into 1-inch balls, then roll in sugar. Place 3 inches apart on prepared cookie sheets. Flatten each ball to ¼-inch thickness with bottom of glass. Bake in batches for 8 to 10 minutes or just until set but still soft and edges are lightly golden; do not overbake. Transfer cookies to rack to cool. Makes about 2 dozen cookies.

measuring
spoons

# REFRIGERATOR

## COOKIES

♦ ♦ ♦

Tropical-tasting cookies studded with coconut and dried pineapple chunks. ♦ Perfect with icy lemonade or iced tea on the porch on a sultry afternoon. ♦ Dried pineapple rings (not the dyed red and green kind for fruitcake) are available at specialty food shops, bulk-food and some health-food stores and supermarkets. Toss the diced pineapple in a little of the flour to keep chunks separate.

pineapple

## PIÑA COLADA COOKIES

½ cup (1 stick) butter, at room temperature
½ cup sugar
2 tablespoons beaten egg
1 teaspoon rum or vanilla
¾ cup plus 2 tablespoons all-purpose flour

¼ teaspoon baking powder
¼ teaspoon baking soda
½ cup sweetened flaked or shredded coconut
½ cup diced dried pineapple rings

CREAM BUTTER and sugar in large bowl of electric mixer. Beat in egg and vanilla, then flour, baking powder, baking soda, and coconut just until thoroughly combined. Stir in diced pineapple.

On large piece of plastic wrap, shape dough into 3-inch-thick roll, enclose in wrap, and chill for 2 hours or until firm enough to slice.

Preheat oven to 350°F. Adjust oven rack to middle position. Cut dough into ¼-inch-thick slices and place 2 inches apart on ungreased cookie sheets. Bake in batches for 6 to 8 minutes or just until set but still soft and edges are browned and crisp. Transfer cookies to rack to cool. Makes about 2 dozen cookies.

## VANILLA SLICES

½ cup (1 stick) butter,
   at room temperature
1 cup sugar or packed
   brown sugar
1 large egg

1 teaspoon vanilla
1 ¾ cups all-purpose flour
1 teaspoon baking powder
¼ teaspoon salt

CREAM BUTTER and sugar in large bowl of electric mixer. Beat in egg and vanilla, then flour, baking powder, and salt just until thoroughly combined.

Shape dough into 2-inch-diameter roll, wrap in plastic wrap, and chill for 2 hours or until firm enough to slice.

Preheat oven to 350°F. Adjust oven rack to middle position. Lightly spray or grease cookie sheets. Cut dough into ⅛-inch-thick slices and place 1 inch apart on prepared cookie sheets. Bake in batches for 6 to 8 minutes or just until set. Transfer cookies to rack to cool. Makes about 3 dozen cookies.

*W*hat used to be called ice-box cookie dough is the secret to making fresh cookies at the drop of a hat. You simply refrigerate or freeze the dough, then thaw before slicing and baking. White sugar produces vanilla slices and brown sugar, butterscotch slices

A bsolutely beautiful and *marvelous and wonderful and chewy and coconutty – and great!*

## CHEWY COCONUT THINS

| | |
|---|---|
| 1 cup (2 sticks) butter, at room temperature | 1½ teaspoons baking powder |
| 1 cup sugar | ½ teaspoon baking soda |
| 1 large egg | 1 cup sweetened flaked or shredded coconut |
| 2 teaspoons vanilla | |
| 1¾ cups all-purpose flour | |

CREAM BUTTER and sugar in large bowl of electric mixer. Beat in egg and vanilla, then flour, baking powder, and baking soda just until thoroughly combined. Stir in coconut.

Form dough into 3-inch roll and wrap in plastic wrap. Refrigerate until firm enough to slice.

Preheat oven to 350°F. Adjust oven rack to middle position.

Cut dough into ¼-inch thick slices and place 2 inches apart on ungreased cookie sheets. Bake in batches for 8 to 10 minutes or just until set but still soft and edges are lightly golden; do not overbake. Transfer cookies to rack to cool. Makes about 3 dozen cookies.

## CHOCOLATE PINWHEEL COOKIES

½ cup (1 stick) butter,
   at room temperature
1 cup sugar
1 large egg
1 teaspoon vanilla
Finely grated zest of
   1 small lemon

1 ¾ cups all-purpose flour
1 teaspoon baking powder
¼ teaspoon salt
1 ounce (1 square)
   unsweetened chocolate,
   melted, cooled

CREAM BUTTER and sugar in large bowl of electric mixer. Beat in egg, vanilla, and lemon zest, then flour, baking powder, and salt just until thoroughly combined. Divide dough in half and stir melted chocolate into one batch. Wrap both in plastic wrap and chill for 1 hour or until firm enough to handle.

Roll each piece to a ⅛-inch-thick rectangle between 2 pieces of plastic wrap or wax paper. Remove plastic wrap and place chocolate dough on top of light dough. Starting with longer side, roll doughs tightly together like a jellyroll. Cut in half to make 2 rolls and wrap in plastic wrap; chill until firm.

Preheat oven to 350°F. Adjust oven rack to middle position. Lightly spray or grease cookie sheets.

Cut dough into ¼-inch-thick slices and place 1 inch apart on prepared cookie sheets. Bake in batches for 8 to 10 minutes or just until set. Transfer cookies to rack to cool. Makes about 3 dozen cookies.

P*retty pinwheels are cookie-jar favorites. ◆ While they're just a little more complicated to make than most cookies, the results are well worth the effort.*

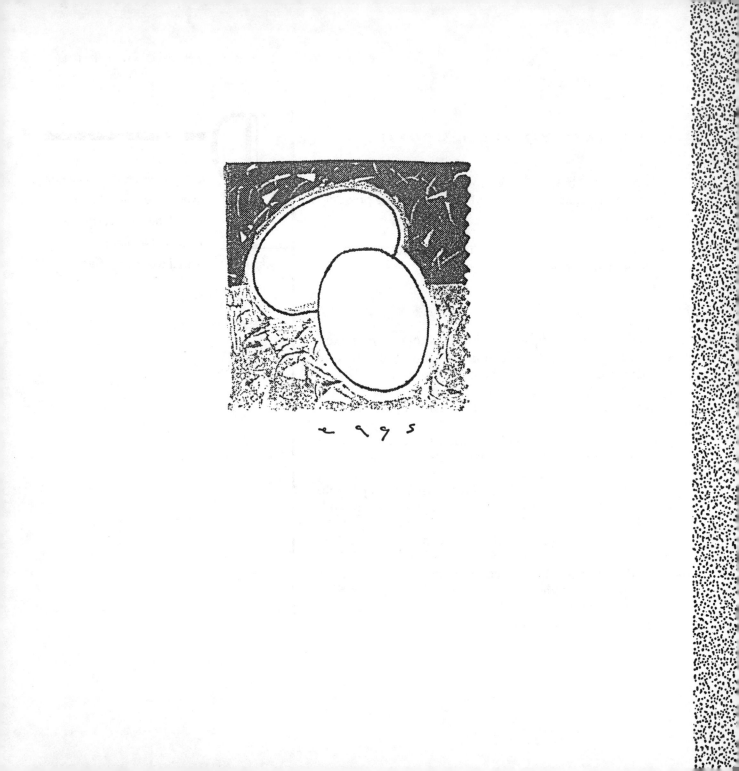

eggs

# B<sup>A</sup>R

COOKIES

♦ ♦ ♦

**F**rom my book, Joie Warner's Apple Desserts, cinnamon-sprinkled apple slices are sandwiched between sweet and buttery oatmeal layers for a totally irresistible bar cookie.

## APPLE OAT SQUARES

1½ cups quick oats (not instant)
1½ cups all-purpose flour
¼ teaspoon baking soda
½ teaspoon salt
1 cup packed brown sugar
¾ cup (1½ sticks) butter, melted, cooled

3 cups peeled, cored, thinly sliced Granny Smith apples
½ teaspoon ground cinnamon
¼ cup sugar
2 tablespoons butter

PREHEAT OVEN to 350°F.
   Stir oats, flour, baking soda, salt, brown sugar, and melted butter in large bowl until thoroughly combined. Press half the mixture evenly into bottom of 9-inch square baking pan. Toss apples, cinnamon, and sugar in bowl, then spread evenly in pan; dot with butter. Sprinkle with remaining oat mixture and bake for 45 minutes or until golden. Cool and cut into squares. Makes about 9 squares.

## Lemon Squares

1 cup all-purpose flour
¼ cup sugar
½ cup (1 stick) butter,
   at room temperature
3 large eggs
1½ cups sugar
Grated zest of 2 medium
   lemons

½ cup fresh lemon juice
⅓ cup all-purpose flour
½ teaspoon baking powder
Confectioners' sugar for
   dusting

PREHEAT OVEN to 350°F. Adjust oven rack to middle position.

Combine 1 cup flour, ¼ cup sugar, and butter in large bowl until crumbly but thoroughly combined. Press dough evenly into ungreased 8-inch square glass baking pan. Bake for 12 to 14 minutes or just until firm but not browned.

Meanwhile, whisk eggs, 1½ cups sugar, lemon zest, and lemon juice in large bowl until blended. Stir in ⅓ cup flour and baking powder until thoroughly combined. Pour lemon mixture over hot crust and bake another 25 minutes or just until topping is set. Remove pan to rack and generously dust with confectioners' sugar, using a tiny sieve. Cool completely, then cover pan and refrigerate. Cut into squares. Makes about 16 squares.

*S*o easy, so lemony, so exquisite! Place lemon squares on your most chic cake stand and, if you like, decorate them with edible flowers such as yellow pansies and purple violets. Serve with your rarest tea (or coffee), or as dessert. ◆ The lemon topping is rather like lemon curd so they are bit difficult to cut neatly – use a good sharp knife. But what they lack in presentation, they more than make up for in flavor!

Most bar cookies are simple, homey confections. Not this cookie! This one's fairly fancy with a layer of preserves – raspberry's terrific but you may use strawberry, peach, apricot, or black currant – sandwiched between a buttery pastry and delicate meringue topping. ◆ For the very best flavor, use homemade jam or the very best-quality preserves. ◆ Don't make Raspberry Meringue Squares on a humid day.

## RASPBERRY MERINGUE SQUARES

1 cup all-purpose flour
¼ cup sugar
½ cup (1 stick) butter, at room temperature
2 large egg whites
¼ teaspoon cream of tartar
⅛ teaspoon salt

1 teaspoon vanilla
⅓ cup sugar
½ cup pecan halves, lightly toasted, finely chopped
½ cup seedless raspberry jam

PREHEAT OVEN to 350°F. Adjust oven rack to middle position.

Combine 1 cup flour, sugar, and butter in medium bowl until crumbly but thoroughly combined. Press dough evenly into ungreased 8-inch square baking pan. Bake for 12 to 15 minutes or just until firm but not browned.

Beat egg whites in large bowl of electric mixer on high speed until very soft peaks form (they tip over slightly). Add cream of tartar, salt, and vanilla and beat several seconds to combine. Beat in sugar, 1 tablespoon at a time, until very stiff peaks form. Gently fold in nuts.

Spread jam over hot crust. Carefully spread meringue over jam. Bake another 15 to 20 minutes or just until topping is lightly golden; watch carefully that it doesn't burn. Cool in pan on rack. Cut into squares. Makes about 16 squares.

## TREASURE BARS

1 cup all-purpose flour
¼ cup sugar
½ cup (1 stick) butter,
    at room temperature
2 large eggs
¾ cup packed brown sugar
1 tablespoon all-purpose
    flour
½ teaspoon baking powder

¼ teaspoon salt
1 teaspoon vanilla
¾ cup chopped dates
½ cup sweetened shredded
    or flaked coconut
½ cup pecan halves,
    chopped
½ cup chocolate chips

PREHEAT OVEN to 350°F. Adjust oven rack to middle position.

Combine 1 cup flour, sugar, and butter in medium bowl until crumbly but thoroughly combined. Press dough evenly into ungreased 8-inch square baking pan. Bake for 12 to 14 minutes or just until firm but not browned.

Meanwhile, whisk eggs, brown sugar, 1 tablespoon flour, baking powder, salt, and vanilla just until thoroughly combined. Stir in dates, coconut, pecans, and chocolate chips. Spread mixture over hot crust and bake another 15 to 20 minutes or just until topping is set but still moist in center. Cool in pan on rack. Cut into bars. Makes about 16 bars.

R ich and satisfying, these bars are topped with tiny treasures – dates, coconut, pecans – and chocolate chips. ◆ Cut them into tiny squares and nestle them in petit-four cups if desired.

Easier to make than a pecan pie and just as sweet and gooey and delicious.
◆ Spread a layer of melted semisweet or bittersweet chocolate between the crust and pecan topping for even more lusciousness. ◆ And why not gild the lily and serve with dollops of lightly whipped cream or vanilla ice cream?

creamer

## PECAN PIE BARS

1 cup all-purpose flour
¼ cup sugar
½ cup (1 stick) butter, at room temperature
2 large eggs
⅓ cup (5⅓ tablespoons) butter, melted, cooled
1 cup packed brown sugar

½ cup corn syrup
1 teaspoon vanilla
Grated zest of 1 medium lemon
¾ cup pecan halves, chopped

PREHEAT OVEN to 350°F. Adjust oven rack to middle position.

Combine flour, sugar, and ½ cup butter in medium bowl until crumbly but thoroughly combined. Press dough evenly into ungreased 9-inch square baking pan. Bake for 12 to 14 minutes or just until firm but not browned.

Meanwhile, whisk eggs, melted butter, brown sugar, corn syrup, vanilla, and lemon zest just until thoroughly combined. Stir in chopped pecans. Spread mixture over hot crust and bake another 15 to 20 minutes or just until topping is set. Cool in pan on rack. Cut into bars. Makes about 16 bars.

# BROWNIES

◆ ◆ ◆

*appiness is a cookie jar filled with peanutty-chocolate brownies.*

## CHOCOLATE PEANUT BUTTER BROWNIES

¼ cup (½ stick) butter, at room temperature
¼ cup chunky peanut butter
1 cup packed brown sugar
2 large eggs
1 teaspoon vanilla

2 ounces (2 squares) unsweetened chocolate, melted, cooled
½ cup all-purpose flour
1 teaspoon baking powder
½ cup chopped peanuts

PREHEAT OVEN to 350°F. Adjust oven rack to middle position. Lightly spray or grease 8-inch square baking pan.
Cream butter, peanut butter, and brown sugar in large bowl of electric mixer. Beat in eggs, vanilla, and melted chocolate just until thoroughly combined. Fold in flour, baking powder, and peanuts. Spread batter evenly in prepared pan. Bake for 15 to 20 minutes or just until tester inserted in center comes out slightly moist; do not overbake. Cool in pan on rack. Cut into squares. Makes about 16 brownies.

# ROCKY ROAD FUDGE BROWNIES

2 large eggs
½ cup (1 stick) butter,
  melted, cooled
2 ounces (2 squares)
  unsweetened chocolate,
  melted, cooled
¾ cup sugar
1 teaspoon vanilla
¾ cup all-purpose flour
¼ teaspoon salt
¼ teaspoon baking powder
½ cup pecan halves or
  walnuts, coarsely
  chopped

16 regular-size
  marshmallows, cut in
  halves or quarters
2 ounces (2 squares)
  unsweetened chocolate
¼ cup (½ stick) butter
1½ cups confectioners'
  sugar
¼ cup half-and-half
1 teaspoon vanilla

PREHEAT OVEN to 350°F. Adjust oven rack to middle position. Lightly spray or grease 9-inch square baking pan.

Beat eggs in large bowl of electric mixer until foamy. Beat in ½ cup melted butter and 2 ounces melted chocolate, sugar, and vanilla, then flour, salt, and baking powder just until thoroughly combined. Stir in nuts.

Spread batter evenly in prepared pan. Bake for 15 to 20 minutes or just until tester inserted in center comes out slightly moist, do not overbake. Remove pan from oven, top with marshmallows, then return to oven for 2 minutes – no longer. Transfer to rack and cool in pan.

Meanwhile, in small heavy saucepan over *very* low heat, melt 2 ounces chocolate and ¼ cup butter. Remove from heat and whisk in confectioners' sugar (if lumpy, sift through a sieve), half-and-half, and vanilla until smooth. Drizzle frosting over top, leaving marshmallows showing here and there. Cool completely. Cut into bars or squares. Makes about 16 brownies.

*F*udge brownies with big chunks of marshmallows and chopped pecans – no wonder they're so popular! ♦ Some cooks will be tempted to use miniature marshmallows, but rocky road aficionados prefer hand cut, large pieces. ♦ Melt the butter and chocolate together in a small heavy saucepan over very low heat.

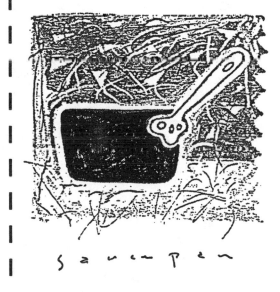

saucepan

T he secret to these marvelously
moist brownies is to under-
bake them – they should be
quite moist. ◆ Melt the butter
and chocolate together in a small heavy
saucepan over very low heat.

## FUDGE CAKE BROWNIES

½ cup (1 stick) butter,
   melted, cooled
2 ounces (2 squares)
   unsweetened chocolate,
   melted, cooled
1 cup sugar

2 large eggs
½ teaspoon vanilla
1 cup pecan halves,
   coarsely chopped
1 cup all-purpose flour

PREHEAT OVEN to 350°F. Adjust oven rack to middle position. Lightly spray or grease 8-inch square baking pan.
   Whisk butter, chocolate, and sugar in large bowl until thoroughly combined. Beat in eggs, vanilla, pecans, and flour until well blended. Spread batter evenly in prepared pan. Bake for 15 minutes or just until almost set and tester inserted in center comes out moist; do not overbake. Cool in pan on rack. Cut into bars. Makes about 16 brownies.

## MARBLED BROWNIE BARS

½ cup (1 stick) butter,
   at room temperature
1 cup sugar
2 large eggs
1 teaspoon vanilla
1 cup all-purpose flour
¼ teaspoon baking powder

¼ teaspoon salt
¼ teaspoon almond extract
2 squares (2 ounces)
   unsweetened chocolate,
   melted, cooled
¼ cup pecan halves,
   coarsely chopped

PREHEAT OVEN to 350°F. Adjust oven rack to middle position. Lightly spray or grease 8-inch square baking pan.

Cream butter and sugar in large bowl of electric mixer. Beat in eggs and vanilla, then flour, baking powder, and salt just until thoroughly combined.

Divide batter in half, stir almond extract into one batch and melted chocolate and nuts into the other.

Drop heaping tablespoonfuls of batter into prepared pan, alternating mounds in a checkerboard pattern. Swirl batters together – don't overdo it – with a knife to marbleize. Bake for 15 to 20 minutes or just until tester inserted in center comes out slightly moist; do not overbake. Cool in pan on rack. Cut into bars. Makes about 16 brownies.

*Two-tone brownies are simply made by dividing the batter in half and adding chocolate to one and almond flavoring to the other, then swirling a knife in the two batters to create an attractive marbleized effect.*

*lond brownies – butterscotch-flavored and slightly chewy – are chock-full of nuts and chocolate chips.*

## BUTTERSCOTCH CHOCOLATE-CHIP BROWNIES

½ cup (1 stick) butter, melted, cooled
1 cup packed brown sugar
1 large egg
1 teaspoon vanilla
1 cup all-purpose flour
1 teaspoon baking powder

½ teaspoon salt
⅓ cup pecan halves, lightly toasted, coarsely chopped
½ cup jumbo-size semisweet chocolate chips

PREHEAT OVEN to 350°F. Adjust oven rack to middle position. Lightly spray or grease 8-inch square baking pan.

Stir melted butter and brown sugar in medium bowl until blended. Stir in egg and vanilla, then flour, baking powder, and salt just until thoroughly combined. Stir in pecans and chocolate chips. Spread batter evenly in prepared pan. Bake for 15 to 20 minutes or just until tester inserted in center comes out slightly moist; do not overbake. Cool in pan on rack. Cut into squares. Makes about 16 brownies.

## FUDGY CHOCOLATE BROWNIES

3 large eggs
⅛ teaspoon salt
1⅔ cups sugar
4 ounces (4 squares)
   semisweet chocolate,
   melted, cooled

½ cup (1 stick) butter,
   melted, cooled
1 teaspoon vanilla
¾ cup all-purpose flour
½ cup pecan halves,
   coarsely chopped

PREHEAT OVEN to 375°F. Adjust oven rack to middle position. Lightly spray or grease 8-inch square baking pan.

Beat eggs and salt in large bowl of electric mixer until foamy. Beat in sugar, 1 tablespoon at a time, until very pale yellow and very thick, about 5 minutes. On low speed, beat in melted chocolate, melted butter, and vanilla, then fold in flour and nuts with rubber spatula. Spread batter evenly in prepared pan. Bake for 25 to 30 minutes or just until tester inserted in center comes out slightly moist; do not overbake. Cool in pan on rack. Cut into bars. Makes about 16 brownies.

*Super-easy to make with a terrific crispy-on-the-outside, fudgy-in-the-center texture. ◆ It's important to let the chocolate and butter cool thoroughly (melt them together over very low heat in a heavy saucepan) and not to overbake or brownies won't be fudgy. ◆ Serve with a big scoop of vanilla ice cream on the side.*

# INDEX

◆ ◆ ◆

## Books in Joie Warner's ALL THE BEST series

----

— *also available* —

----

Available from
HEARST/WILLIAM MORROW